The Greater St. Petersburg and Clearwater Area Bucket List
100 ways to have a True 'Sunshine City' Experience

If you haven't visited this part of Florida, you are really missing If you haven't visited this part of Florida, you are really missing out. Of course, the area had a reputation for being strictly for retirees, but this isn't your grandparents Greater St. Petersburg area. Times have certainly changed, with and diverse a mixed age group now living in the area, with a creative and artistic vibe permeating the entire area. You will now encounter a creative food scene, live music venues, craft breweries and dozens of creative souls working in many different medians and styles of art. The one thing that hasn't changed is the natural beauty you will discover along the 35 miles of Gulf coastline. Almost endless parks, nature preserves, water activities and wildlife encounters make this area a mix of city sophistication with natural beauty seemingly never too far away. The Greater St Petersburg/ Clearwater area has a little bit of everything for everyone from age 1 to 100, and every age in between.

We hope you use this list as an introduction to the wonderful activities this amazing area has to offer. Keep in mind this is just our list and an introduction, with input from locals, tourists, and our personal experience with numerous visits over the years. Everyone will have their own styles and tastes, so if our list doesn't exactly align with yours that's fine. We look forward to your area guide being written and published. Feel free to send us a copy of your version once it is available. We look forward to reading it! We are always looking for new things to experience in the Greater St. Petersburg/ Clearwater area!

No matter what time of year you visit, you will find so many things to do, plan ahead and prioritize the things you really want to see, do and visit to maximize your time. Of course, that's why you bought the Bucket List Book, so put it to good use and enjoy your visit!

"All the Best" Larry

Cover Photo Credits: IrisImages anddigidrean courtesy of the Author.

GW00499148

CONTENTS

CATCH THE SUNSET OVER CLEARWATER BEACH

WHAT'S THE DEAL: If you only do 1 thing while visiting the gulf coast, see an unobstructed sunset from a signature local beach. Chances are, it might be the most unforgettable sunset you will ever experience!

DO IT IF: You want to see the 'green flash' when the sun sets below the horizon. Or just enjoy seeing the setting sun disappear below the water line, marking the end of the day.

SKIP IT IF: You hate sand in your sandals or are more of a sunrise person.

LOCAL ADVICE: Watching the sunset is a very popular past time during the busy season in Clearwater. (January – April). Give yourself plenty of time to arrive at the beach and find parking, based on the actual sunset time!

I DID IT: ☐ www.timeanddate.com/sun/usa/clearwater

DID YOU KNOW?

Sunset times vary widely throughout the year, so check the times to arrive in time. From as early as 5:35 pm in December to as late as 8:31 pm in June, there is an almost 3-hour sunset time difference throughout the year. Don't be late or you could miss the "Green Flash."

WATCH DOLPHINS IN
THEIR NATURAL HABITAT

WHAT'S THE DEAL? There are numerous bay cruises and Dolphin watch tours where you can see these amazing mammals up close and personal.

DO IT IF: You enjoy Mother Nature's creatures viewed in their natural habitats.

SKIP IT IF: You prefer the convenience of the local aquarium, or your dolphin spotting is limited to re-runs of flipper.

LOCAL ADVICE: There are many companies offering Dolphin watches in the area. Whichever one you chose, book early during high season because space is limited, and dolphins are popular. Lil Toot is a fun boat for kids and have been doing dolphin watch cruises for over 20 years, so they know where to find the playful dolphins as they make their way around the Gulf of Mexico.

I DID IT: ☐ www.littletoot.us

DID YOU KNOW?

Dolphins eat fish, squid, and crustaceans. They do not chew their food but may break it into smaller pieces before swallowing. Dolphins have an array of vocalizations such as clicks, whistles and squeals which they use for their well-developed communication and echolocation skills.

ISLAND HOP LIKE A BUCCANEER

WHAT'S THE DEAL? If you want to truly enjoy a carefree adventure, rent your own boat, and explore the small, uninhabited islands that dot the coastline.

DO IT IF: You really have a sense of adventure and independence. Also, if you can read a navigational chart.

SKIP IT IF: You get lost looking for your car at the local Walmart.

LOCAL ADVICE: Once again there are numerous rental options, but reserve ahead during high season. Blind pass is a centrally located launching spot for your island-hopping adventure. You will have access shell key to the south as well as numerous sandbars in the area to get away from it all. You will need a Florida boaters license which can be attained at check in and must be 25 years or older to rent the boat.

I DID IT: ☐ www.blindpassboatandjetski.com/boat-rentals

DID YOU KNOW?

The Johns Pass sandbar is located in the western part of Boca Ciega Bay. It's just inland from Johns Pass Inlet, northeast of Johns Pass bridge. It's roughly between Treasure Island and Madeira Beach. There are other islands in Boca Ciega Bay, as well, including Little Bird Key, Eleanor Island and Archie's Island.

SCOOT AROUND

WHAT'S THE DEAL? There is no shortage of wheels you can rent to get you quickly around town.

DO IT IF: If you prefer a set of wheels to get you where you are going!

SKIP IT IF: You are in no rush and walking is your preferred mode of transportation.

LOCAL ADVICE: There are a lot of options when it comes to rentals around the greater St Petersburg area. From 2 wheeled scooters, kick-push scooters to slingshots and even mobility scooters, you have many options getting you around downtown or to the beach.

I DID IT: ☐ www.droptopcarrentals.com

DID YOU KNOW?

A scooter boom took place in USA during the 1930s. In the United States, scooters first enjoyed wide popularity during the Great Depression. At that time, many children built their own scooters from recycled wood. This promoted a level of freedom and mobility for those who can't afford to buy cars.

ROOT ON THE RAYS

WHAT'S THE DEAL? Starting as an expansion team in 1998, originally known as the Devil Rays, the Tampa Bay Rays is the local team competing in Major League Baseball.

DO IT IF: You enjoy rooting on the local team competing at the highest level.

SKIP IT IF: The pace of baseball is a bit slow for you.

LOCAL ADVICE: The Rays home games are played in St. Petersburg at "the Trop." Crowd size will vary depending on who the visiting teams might be. Plan ahead for tickets if the visiting team is a popular northern ball club like the Red Sox, Cubs or Yankees.

I DID IT: ☐   www.mlb.com/rays

DID YOU KNOW?

Although the Rays have never won a world series, they have had some great ball players over the years. Some of their best include Hall of Famer Wade Boggs, Tampa's own, Fred McGriff, David Price, Carl Crawford, Evan Longoria and the pride of Rhode Island, Rocco Baldelli.

STAY AT THE PINK PALACE

WHAT'S THE DEAL? Since its Grand Opening in the heyday of the Great Gatsby Era in 1928, The Don Cesar has been welcoming travelers for nearly a century. Once high society's playground with celebrities from the silver screen and athletes from a past era, the Don has always been a Gulf Coast icon. The Don Cesar boasts a rich and glamorous history that you can personally experience.

DO IT IF: You wish to stay in a 1920's era grand Gulf front hotel, found on the National Register of Historic Places.

SKIP IT IF: Modern boutique accommodations are what you prefer.

LOCAL ADVICE: You only live once so book a beach front suite and enjoy stunning views and sunsets directly from your Gulf Front Balcony! The "Don" offers bi-level penthouse suites and their signature Boca Ciega Presidential Suite. Trust us, you'll enjoy it!

I DID IT: ☐   www.doncesar.com

DID YOU KNOW?

Hotel founder Thomas Rowe suffered a heart attack and died suddenly in the lobby and his estranged wife, Mary, inherits the hotel, in 1940. According to local lore, Rowe's spirit still walks the halls of his beloved Pink Palace.

7

SEE THE SPONGE DOCKS

WHAT'S THE DEAL? By 1890, the sponge industry was firmly established in Tarpon Springs. The Cheney Sponge Company sold almost a million dollars' worth of sponges that year alone. Over the next few years, experienced divers from Greece were brought to Tarpon Springs. By using rubberized diving suits and helmets, they increased harvests. By 1905, over 500 Greek sponge divers were at work, using more than 50 boats.

DO IT IF: You want to see what Florida looked like before developers got their hands on it and want to learn about 19th century Florida history.

SKIP IT IF: The sight of a sponge diving suit given you claustrophobic shivers.

LOCAL ADVICE: The sponge docks in Tarpon Springs and the influence of Greek immigrants can still be felt in the area. It is truly one of the most unique cultural locations in all of Florida and deserves a visit.

I DID IT: ☐ spongedocks.net

DID YOU KNOW?

Natural sponges are still harvested, sold, and used today, though with more of a focus on sustainability than before. Sponges are a renewable resource in that they can regrow when a piece is removed. However, roughly 90% of sponges sold currently are the synthetic type.

9

DELIGHT IN DALI

WHAT'S THE DEAL? Visit one of the most wide-ranging art collections of famed and iconic Spanish painter and illustrator, Salvadore Dali. He was truly one of the world's most famous and recognized artists of all time.

DO IT IF: You wish to see the Girl with Curls among other famous Dali works in person.

SKIP IT IF: The image of melting watches freaks you out. (Although that famous Dali painting hangs in the MOMA in New York.)

LOCAL ADVICE: The Dali Museum in Downtown St. Petersburg is truly a world class exhibit of the famous surrealist Spanish artist. They have more than 2400 exhibits spanning multiple forms of expression including oil paintings, illustration, photography and even some personal items once belonging to the famed artist. Timed tickets are required for entry so book ahead.

I DID IT: ☐ thedali.org

DID YOU KNOW?

The famous "melting watches" that appear in "The Persistence of Memory" suggest Einstein's theory that time is relative and not fixed. Dalí later claimed that the idea for clocks functioning symbolically in this way came to him when he was contemplating Camembert cheese.

WANDER THE PIER

WHAT'S THE DEAL? Explore one of the most iconic spots in downtown St. Petersburg, the recently renovated Peir, where you'll find something for everyone.

DO IT IF: You like semi-touristy shopping and restaurant areas, of course with amazing views of the bay.

SKIP IT IF: You prefer to avoid touristy areas at all costs.

LOCAL ADVICE: There is really something for everyone along the pier. From waterfront shopping, casual dining with amazing views, a playground, local sculpture, a museum, splashpad and even a beach, you could literally spend a day exploring here. Keep an eye out for the Red Pelicans, a symbol of St. Petersburg, welcoming you to the pier.

I DID IT: ☐ stpetepier.org

DID YOU KNOW?

The Orange Belt Railway built the Railroad Pier which extended a half-mile into Tampa Bay from the foot of 1st Ave S, the terminus of the railroad. Lined with warehouses and loading docks, the 3,000 ftlong structure soon became popular with anglers and swimmers, prompting the construction of a bathing pavilion and toboggan slide.

LOOK FOR "LITTLE COOPERSTOWN"

WHAT'S THE DEAL? The St. Petersburg Museum of History has designed two prime rooms to display his World's Largest Collection of Autographed Baseballs.

DO IT IF: You love the history of the baseball and autograph collecting is right up your alley.

SKIP IT IF: No time for baseballs, I'm off to the beach.

LOCAL ADVICE: Paying homage to the local love and lore of baseball, The Museum had put together an impressive collection of more than 5,000 signed baseballs. Keep in mind it isn't just ball players who have signed over the years, with autographs from actors, singers, and politicians as well.

I DID IT: ☐ spmoh.com

DID YOU KNOW?

The collection began in 1956 at Yankees spring training with a signed baseball from Mickey Mantle. Little Cooperstown houses baseballs signed by immortal players like Babe Ruth, Shoeless Joe Jackson, Lou Gehrig, Ted Williams and Joe DiMaggio, Marilyn Monroe, and several U.S. presidents, Richard Nixon, Barack Obama, and Ronald Reagan.

MARVEL AT MURALS

WHAT'S THE DEAL? Spread out throughout many neighborhoods in downtown St. Peterburg, you'll be amazed by massive and stunning wall art.

DO IT IF: You admire creative and colorful works of art on a massive scale.

SKIP IT IF: Art by your definition must be framed and hanging on the wall of a museum.

LOCAL ADVICE: There are more than 600 murals throughout the greater downtown St. Petersburg area, so if there is a bare wall surface, chances are there is a mural adorning it. There are maps available online to help guide you and even bike and walking tours if you prefer a guide and direction.

I DID IT: ☐ stpetemuraltour.com/map-of-st-pete-murals
www.stpetebikingtours.com

DID YOU KNOW?

It all started around 2010, when city officials loosened a local ban on street art, instead embracing local artists and their vision of transforming St. Petersburg into a true arts destination. There's even an annual mural festival each October, which brings artists from around the world to St. Pete to create massive works of public art for all to enjoy.

SEE SOME AMAZING SANDCASTLES

WHAT'S THE DEAL? Considered the Super Bowl of sandcastle competition, the sanding ovation master cup brings in the best sand artists from around the globe.

DO IT IF: You delight in the creativity these amazing artists mold from beach sand.

SKIP IT IF: Sand is best used for in a box for kids to play in.

LOCAL ADVICE: Come see Treasure Island's beach come to life at Sanding Ovations. You won't believe the things they can create when master sculptors use their imaginations and turn piles of sand and buckets of water into "OUTSANDING" works of art!

I DID IT: ☐ sandingovationsmasterscup.com

DID YOU KNOW?

Florida Governor Jeb Bush proclaimed Treasure Island as the Sand Sculpture Capital of Florida in 2001. This is what helped lead to the creation of Sanding Ovations. Master sand sculptors from around the world come to Treasure Island to create sand masterpieces for everyone to enjoy.

SEEK OUT CIVIL HISTORY

WHAT'S THE DEAL? Believe it or not, the greater St. Petersburg area still has remnants from the U.S. civil war.

DO IT IF: You like to delve deep into local history or a real civil war buff.

SKIP IT IF: You are more of an American Revolution fan.

LOCAL ADVICE: Union forces captured Egmont Key in July 1861 and used it as a base for attacks on Confederate ships and positions in the Tampa area. The Union also used the island as a military prison and a refuge for southern pro-Union sympathizers. A cemetery for Union and Confederate dead was opened on the island in 1864. The island is currently a state park and is only accessible by boat. Only half of the island is open to the public, the south side is a protected bird sanctuary.

I DID IT: ☐ www.florida-guidebook.com/egmont-key

DID YOU KNOW?

Through the years, Egmont Key has been home to two lighthouses, a fort, a movie theater, a cemetery, boat pilots, and a radio beacon. Today, all that remains on the island is a truncated lighthouse, crumbling remains of the fort, a small colony of gopher tortoises, and a park ranger to interpret the island's history.

14

FIND THE OLD
KRESS BUILDING

WHAT'S THE DEAL? Five and Dime stores were found everywhere throughout America during the late 1800's until the middle part of the 20th Century. S.H. Kress had a vision to build ornamental and beautiful buildings for the American shopper to enjoy. The S. H. Kress and Co. Building is located at 475 Central Avenue and the corner of 5th Street and was built in 1927.

DO IT IF: Really love the look of Beaux- Arts buildings.

SKIP IT IF: You prefer more of Spanish Revival design.

LOCAL ADVICE: The Kress building is just one of more than 300 historic and preserved structures located in the downtown St. Petersburg historic district. Also in the area is the former Pennsylvania Hotel, now a Courtyard and the First United Methodist Church.

I DID IT: [ ] kressbuildingstpetefl.com

DID YOU KNOW?

Like the Kress 'five and dime' in St. Petersburg, many of the S.H. Kress buildings around the United States are so beautiful and historic, many have been repurposed into condos, restaurants, hotels, and even Night Clubs.

TRY A TAIL GRAB VULCAN

WHAT'S THE DEAL? The almost always present strong winds and shallow warm waters make this area one of the best in the world for kite boarding or kite surfing.

DO IT IF: You want to try a new sport on the water while getting some amazing exercise at the same time.

SKIP IT IF: Being able to hold the kite and flying through the air may be physically difficult for you.

LOCAL ADVICE: If this is something you have always wanted to try but didn't know where to start, look no further. Lessons and equipment are available to begin your journey and learn one of the most exhilarating water sports on the planet.

I DID IT: ☐ sakitesurfadventures.com

DID YOU KNOW?

Two brothers, Bruno Legaignoux and Dominique Legaignoux, from the Atlantic coast of France, developed kites for kitesurfing in the late 1970s and early 1980s and patented an inflatable kite design in November 1984.

KAYAK CALADESI ISLAND

WHAT'S THE DEAL? A small Island just off the coast of Dunedin is only accessible by boat and kayak is the most efficient option for you to explore the State Park.

DO IT IF: You like paddling through shallow water, seeing local wildlife and unspoiled mangroves.

SKIP IT IF: Remote islands and unspoiled nature areas that are hard to get to are not your style.

LOCAL ADVICE: One of the best ways to experience Caladesi Island is to take the paddling trail, which begins and ends at the park's marina and café. The trail begins by winding through an extensive mangrove forest. As you approach the entrance, it is shaded by a canopy of branches overhead, which almost seem to form tunnels. The water is often clear over white sand with the trail exiting to shallow seagrass flats, where you may encounter manta rays and pink roseate spoonbills.

I DID IT: ☐ www.floridastateparks.org/parks-and-trails/caladesi-island-state-park

DID YOU KNOW?

> In the 1880s, homesteader Henry Scharrer and his daughter Myrtle lived on the island. Later in life, at the age of 87, Myrtle Scharrer Betz penned the book Yesteryear I Lived in Paradise, telling of her life on the barrier island.

ENJOY A FLORIDA ORANGE IPA

WHAT'S THE DEAL? With the proliferation of craft breweries, St Petersburg, and Clearwater offer many local flavors and styles for you to sample.

DO IT IF: You like to try as many local craft beers as you can get your hands on.

SKIP IT IF: Only the mainstream and large traditional breweries will do for your tastes.

LOCAL ADVICE: 3 daughters was founded by a group of friends and family who had known each other for decades, and all these years later, it's the same crew keeping one of Florida's largest independent and family-owned breweries going and innovating. Visit their Tasting Room in St. Petersburg, or find their craft beers in stores, restaurants, and bars throughout Florida and regionally throughout the south.

I DID IT: ☐ 3dbrewing.com

DID YOU KNOW?

Overall U.S. beer volume sales were up 1% in 2021, while craft brewer volume sales grew 8%, raising small and independent brewers' share of the U.S. beer market by volume to 13.1%.

18

SAMPLE SMOKED FISH

WHAT'S THE DEAL? Ted Peters in south St Petersburg has been serving up smoked fish for more than 70 years.

DO IT IF: You crave locally caught local fresh fish, cooked over a fire of Red Oak.

SKIP IT IF: You are a carnivore.

LOCAL ADVICE: The first restaurant opened in the late 1940's with an open smoker so that people driving by could see and smell the fish spread out on the smoking trays. Ted knew that just as the sun and sand drew tourists to Saint Petersburg Beach, the smell of his fish smoking would bring customers to his restaurant. Many return visitors claim the food still tastes the same when their grandparents first took them there in the 1950's.

I DID IT: ☐ tedpetersfish.com

DID YOU KNOW?

The smoking process typically takes 4 to 6 hours depending on the thickness of the fillet. Originally it was just mullet and spanish mackerel, but the current menu also offers Salmon and Mahi-Mahi.

19

BAR HOP ST. PETE'S COOLEST STREET

WHAT'S THE DEAL?   Downtown St. Petersburg has a vibrant nightclub and bar district, primarily along multiple blocks of Central Avenue.

DO IT IF: You love to grove to live music, find craft cocktails as well as dance to the musical creations of a DJ.

SKIP IT IF: Happy Hour is more your style and you are in bed by 10pm, ironically the time many of the clubs start to ramp up.

LOCAL ADVICE: There are bar, nightclub, live music venues and craft beer hangouts all along Central Avenue for all tastes and desires. The 200 block is the perfect place for barhopping from local favorite Mastry's to the hip Mandarin Hide to the laid-back atmosphere at The Crafty Squirrel. A little further down the avenue is a jazz club called the Independent, and the Grand Central Brew House. Club 201 at the Detroit is a newer spot that offers craft cocktails, live music with a 1920's feel.

I DID IT: ☐   www.visitstpeteclearwater.com/central-ave

DID YOU KNOW?

Obviously, there is no shortage of adult activities along St. Petersburg's Central Avenue. Please drink responsibly if you partake in the consumption of adult beverages and remember to pace yourself. Some of St. Pete's bars and nightclubs are open until 3 am!

21

STAY RIGHT ON THE SAND

WHAT'S THE DEAL? To truly have a unique and carefree vacation, why not stay at a gulf front resort, directly on the beach.

DO IT IF: You want as few hassles as possible while maximizing your beach time.

SKIP IT IF: You prefer to save a few bucks by staying miles away from the beach, packing the car, dealing with traffic, and searching for parking is the kind of vacation you want.

LOCAL ADVICE: If the resort idea sounds good to you, Tradewinds and Rumfish, are an excellent option. There are multiple pools, ocean view rooms, waterfront dining and bars with the Gulf of Mexico waters just a short walk from your hotel room door.

I DID IT: ☐   www.tradewindsresort.com

DID YOU KNOW?

TradeWinds Island Resorts includes Island Grand Beach Resort, the largest beachfront resort in St. Pete Beach, and RumFish Beach Resort by TradeWinds, home of the popular RumFish Grill restaurant. The properties function as two independent resorts, with the "stay at one, play at two" concept. Win-Win!

21

SEE THE GRAND PRIX

WHAT'S THE DEAL?   Since 1985, race cars have been speeding around the streets of downtown St Petersburg and even a runway of Albert Whitted airport.

DO IT IF: You crave the roar of the Indy Cars, up close and personal.

SKIP IT IF: You only do NASCAR.

LOCAL ADVICE: The Firestone Grand Prix of St. Petersburg is an IndyCar Series race held in St. Petersburg, Florida. In most years since 2009, the race has served as the season opener for Gran Prix racing in the U.S. If you haven't seen an open wheel race in person, you should check it out. It's truly amazing how fast the cars can go in a short space.

I DID IT: ☐   www.gpstpete.com

DID YOU KNOW?

The top 5 most important races for fans are the Indianapolis 500, Long Beach, Road America, Laguna Seca, and St. Petersburg. INDYCAR fans are happy with the mix of tracks (street, road & oval) and believe they provide the best test of a driver's talent.

22

REJOICE WITH RESCUED ANIMALS

WHAT'S THE DEAL? Clearwater Marine Aquarium staff and volunteers work each day to rescue marine life and provide the most advanced and effective care to maximize the opportunity to return sick or injured animals to their homes. The animals that come through our doors arrive because they are suffering from an illness or severe injury. Many of our animals are found by local residents, fishermen, park rangers or even visitors to the area.

DO IT IF: It warms your heart to visit mother nature's creatures on the road to recovery!

SKIP IT IF: You are related to "The Grinch."

LOCAL ADVICE: A majority of the resident animals cannot be released due to a variety of reasons, so you will see them in permanent habitats and learn their rescue stories. You'll also see a number of animals receiving daily medical care or undergoing rehabilitation in a working animal hospital.

I DID IT: ☐ www.cmaquarium.org

DID YOU KNOW?

Many of the dolphins and other marine life you may encounter here, often become susceptible to entanglement and ingestion of fishing line or other gear that can cause them to become injured, sick and even potentially lead to their death. To all fishermen, please don't throw your lines, hooks or lead weights into the ocean or gulf, it effects the fragile marine eco system.

FIND FORT DESOTO

WHAT'S THE DEAL? When you arrive, you'll find the largest park within the Pinellas County Park System. Fort De Soto Park consists of 1,136 acres made up of five interconnected islands or keys. These keys are home to beach plants, mangroves, wetlands, palm hammocks, hardwoods, and scores of native plants. Each of these species plays a vital role in the preservation and protection of the natural environment.

DO IT IF: You live for unspoiled nature parks, with dozens of birds and plant species.

SKIP IT IF: You must be withing walking distance of your hotel pool and cocktail service.

LOCAL ADVICE The keys are connected by either bridge or a causeway. You'll find 2 fishing piers, beaches, picnic area, hiking trails, bicycling trails, kayak trail, and a ferry to Egmont Key State Park is available. There is a fee to enter the park but arrive by bike or with a handicap permit and it's free.

I DID IT: ☐ pinellas.gov/parks/fort-de-soto-park

DID YOU KNOW?

The park property was first purchased from the federal government in 1938 for $12,500. In 1941 the property was sold back to the federal government for $18,404 to be used as a gunnery and bombing range during World War II. The property was repurchased from the United States in 1948 for $26,500.

PEDAL ACROSS PINELLAS

WHAT'S THE DEAL? You can ride more than 45 miles from St Petersburg in the south all the way to Tarpon Springs in the south.

DO IT IF: You never met a bike path you did not like.

SKIP IT IF: Pedaling a bicycle is physically difficult or just isn't something you enjoy.

LOCAL ADVICE: This rail trail is without a doubt one of the most popular and well used bike path throughout all of Florida. It literally passes through almost all of Pinellas County, touching 10 towns along the way. It is so useful that some local residents even use the Fred Marquis Pinellas Trail to bike to work and leave the car at home.

I DID IT: ☐   pinellas.gov/pinellas-county-trail-guide

DID YOU KNOW?

When local railroads abandoned more than 34 miles of track in the 1980's, Pinellas County acquired the land for a multi-purpose path. The Pinellas Trail is named after Fred Marquis, a former Pinellas County Administrator who served from 1979 until 2000.

GAZE AT AMAZING GLASS

WHAT'S THE DEAL? The Imagine Museum features a spectacular collection of contemporary glass art from around the globe. You can see firsthand the evolution of the glass art movement by artists who have turned it into contemporary artworks of color, motion, and light.

DO IT IF: You are in awe what artists can create with the medium of molten silica.

SKIP IT IF: The beach is calling...

LOCAL ADVICE: There are more than 500 individually lit glass pieces in over 34,000 square feet of museum space. If you are feeling overwhelmed, and aren't sure where to start, don't fear, The Imagine Museum also offers guided tours. If you have a hard to shop for friend, Imagine Museum also has a gift shop where you can purchase some unique works and take something home for you or someone special.

I DID IT: ☐   www.imaginemuseum.com

DID YOU KNOW?

Harvey Littleton was an American glass artist and is often referred to as the "Father of the Studio Glass Movement". Born in Corning, New York, he grew up in the shadow of Corning Glass Works, where his father headed Research and Development during the 1930s.

TANGLE WITH A TARPON

WHAT'S THE DEAL? If you are looking for an exhilarating day of fishing, nothing quite matches with hooking and trying to reel in a Tarpon.

DO IT IF: You enjoy being out on the water matching your wits and strength against a prized game fish.

SKIP IT IF: The only fish you want is cooked and served on a plate.

LOCAL ADVICE: March to June annually is typically the best time of year for Tarpon fishing. There is usually a large migration with schools of Tarpon swimming south, with sizes ranging from 70 up to over 200 pounds. The best option to land a trophy Tarpon is to sail with an experienced captain. Tarpon is one fish you will want to tangle with but will most likely catch and release. Tarpon are rarely eaten because they have small bones and are difficult to clean to make them edible.

I DID IT: ☐ fishingbooker.com

DID YOU KNOW?

Florida tarpon primary feed on sardines, shrimp, crabs, mullet, pinfish, catfish, needlefish, and will also scavenge the bottom for smaller dead fish. Tarpon have evolved, they are one of the few fish in the world that have a swim bladder. It acts as a lung so they can breathe raw air or extract oxygen through gills.

STEP INTO THE "FRAY"

WHAT'S THE DEAL? There are many options if you are looking for your donut fix. There is one local favorite that always hits the spot.

DO IT IF: You crave a sweet treat and only a donut will do.

SKIP IT IF: You are on a diet.

LOCAL ADVICE: The original Fray's has been serving up donuts to the Greater St. Petersburg community since 1993. The use the freshest ingredients and hand make their selections daily. We recommend the chocolate frosted with the touch of whip cream, our personal favorite. And seniors, remember, you get a free coffee and donut on your birthday.

I DID IT: ☐   www.fraysdonut.com

DID YOU KNOW?

The more than 25,000 donuts shops across our nation serve more than 10 billion donuts each year. And the average American eats 31 donuts a year, which means we each consume two or three donuts a month. Plus, 37% of us eat at least one donut month.

28

SEE HISTORY
BY CANDLELIGHT

WHAT'S THE DEAL? Explore a 1920's neighborhood by candlelight while supporting a local charity.

DO IT IF: Craftsman style bungalows by candlelight entice you.

SKIP IT IF: Walking through an old neighborhood, especially at night, is not for you.

LOCAL ADVICE: The candlelight walk features homes built during the Roaring '20s. You will be transported back in time back over 100 years to when St. Petersburg and the flourishing Old Northeast neighborhood was just beginning to "roar." This is one of the best preserved 1920's neighbor hoods in all the southeastern United States.

I DID IT: ☐ honna.org

DID YOU KNOW?

The historic Old Northeast district borders downtown and boasts nearly 3,000 historic buildings within its borders. The architecture is a mix of Mediterranean and craftsman style bungalows in a tropical setting plentiful with jacarandas, pines, palms, and mature magnolias.

SPIKE IT ON THE SAND

WHAT'S THE DEAL? Beach volleyball is a popular activity with venues throughout the entire area for you to participate with a beach spike of your own.

DO IT IF: You enjoy a fun outdoor beach activity which will certainly get your heart pumping. Watch out for the team of Benny and the Sets if you do some pickup beach volleyball. They're lethal!

SKIP IT IF: You don't know 3 other people to get a game of beach volleyball started.

LOCAL ADVICE: So seriously, if you don't know anyone who plays, sand or beach volleyball, no problem. There are plenty of local courts for pickup games, with all skill levels from novice to pro. There are multiple options both in town and on the beach. Our local beach volleyball expert, Bennett, recommends North Shore Park, Rec Dec, and Post Card Inn on St. Pete Beach. Either way get out and play!

I DID IT: ☐ www.stpeteparksrec.org/northshorepark

DID YOU KNOW?

Beach volleyball was born on the beaches of southern California in the early 20th century. It finally reached the Olympics in 1996 with the U.S. men's tandem taking home the gold medal. The popular women's team of Misty Mae-Traenor and Kerri Walsh Jennings have claimed the gold 3 times.

GLIDE OVER THE GULF

WHAT'S THE DEAL? You want to fly like a bird with amazing views of the beautiful Gulf of Mexico.

DO IT IF: Soaring like an Osprey is what you enjoy.

SKIP IT IF: You are scared to death of heights.

LOCAL ADVICE: One of the most popular gulf activities is parasailing. If offers an exhilarating ride with unparalleled views and can be enjoyed by people 6 and older and weighing less than 265 pounds and not pregnant. This is another popular Gulf Coast activity and there are multiple vendors offering parasailing. Book ahead during busy season and check the weather. High winds and or thunderstorms in the area will cancel the activity.

I DID IT: ☐ www.proparasail.com

DID YOU KNOW?

Parasailing is a low-risk activity. Use an experienced operator who maintains and inspects his equipment on a regular basis. According to Federal Aviation Administration guidelines, your flight will not be higher than 500 vertical feet above the ground. Before you go, make sure the parasail operator is reputable.

31

AMBLE ALONG OSPREY TRAIL

WHAT'S THE DEAL? If you are looking for a spot to see majestic Ospreys in their natural habitat, we have the place for you.

DO IT IF: You are up for a hike to explore an unspoiled wildlife habitat.

SKIP IT IF: Hiking is hard on your knees.

LOCAL ADVICE: This unspoiled gem doesn't receive the same amount of publicity as other nature trails in the St. Petersburg area, but perhaps it should. Just west of Dunedin, hidden amongst the pines are dozens of Osprey nests. Looks for a tangle of twigs hanging down from the top of the pines. Another treat while hiking the trail is the occasional gopher tortoise, digging a burrow to lay eggs.

I DID IT: ☐ floridahikes.com/honeymoonisland

DID YOU KNOW?

Ospreys possess a large, five-foot wingspan and have brown, black, and white coloration throughout their wings and bodies and survive solely on fish. These birds of prey are noted for their nests which are built on tall, open tree branches or poles near the water.

32

JOURNEY TO
JOHN'S PASS

WHAT'S THE DEAL? A pirate, John Levique, made the first passage through the newly created pass. Hence the name, Johns Pass. Located on the waterfront at Johns Pass, this quaint turn-of-the-century fishing village is a popular Pinellas County tourist attraction.

DO IT IF: Shopping dining and water borne activities in 1 convenient location are what you desire.

SKIP IT IF: You prefer to travel across town to find these activities.

LOCAL ADVICE: John's pass is truly Madeira Beaches' 1 stop spot for shops, restaurants, and family entertainment. If fish is what you crave, our personal favorite is the Friendly Fisherman, featuring fresh locally caught seafood. You are so close to the water; you may even spot a dolphin or two swimming by.

I DID IT: ☐ johnspassvillage.net

DID YOU KNOW?

In 1848, John Levique decided to take a load of turtles to New Orleans. When he returned to Florida, he found that the shoreline was changed by a large hurricane, splitting an island in two, exactly in the spot where he had hidden his treasure. Levique sailed his boat through the new pass into Boca Ciega Bay, the new channel was forever known as John's Pass.

GOLF THE GULF

WHAT'S THE DEAL? The Greater St. Petersburg and Clearwater area has no shortage of championship and resort courses, where you can tee off with spectacular views.

DO IT IF: You enjoy Golf in a tropical setting.

SKIP IT IF: Golf is too stressful, I am on vacation to relax.

LOCAL ADVICE: Of course, many of the elite golf courses in the area are private country clubs. The best public option would be Mangrove Bay in St. Petersburg. It has a fun layout and challenges golfers of all skill levels with lots of water hazards. They also have a driving range, and the price will not break the bank. For a true golf vacation, stay at the Innisbrook Resort in Palm Harbor, home of the PGA's Valspar Championship.

I DID IT: ☐ www.golfstpete.com
www.innisbrookgolfresort.com

DID YOU KNOW?

The Innisbrook resort is home to four outstanding courses, including the top-rated Copperhead Course, home of the PGA TOUR's Valspar Championship each March, and a favorite among some of the world's finest golf professionals. You can only play the course if you are staying at the resort.

TRY THE TIKIS ON TREASURE ISLAND

WHAT'S THE DEAL? With almost a dozen gulf front tiki bars along 1 stretch of sand, try them all and determine which one is your favorite.

DO IT IF: You love a local tiki bar for happy hour, live music, and sunset.

SKIP IT IF: You came to the Gulf for a more elegant dining experience

LOCAL ADVICE: Pace yourself if you plan to carry out this bucket list item. There are more than a handful of tikis on Treasure Island and extending along St. Pete beach for you to try. We have always enjoyed twisted tiki where it is happy hour all day, but honestly, try them all and decide for yourself!

I DID IT: ☐ twistedtikistpetebeach.com

DID YOU KNOW?

One of the earliest of what is now known as a tiki bar was named "Don the Beachcomber," created in Hollywood , CA. in 1933 by Ernest Gantt (who later legally changed his name to "Donn Beach"). The bar served a wide variety of exotic rum drinks. It displayed many artifacts that he had collected on earlier trips through the tropics and featured a Polynesian theme.

35

EXPLORE THE VAULTS

WHAT'S THE DEAL? The Museum of Fine Arts in St. Petersburg offers a unique experience for art lovers to explore on their own.

DO IT IF: You want to see small works of art at close range.

SKIP IT IF: Only giant wall size murals will do.

LOCAL ADVICE: This fourth iteration of Explore the Vaults features pieces from the museum's permanent collection, specifically paintings known as "cabinet pictures" and small works on paper. The small paintings are best seen close up to show the artist's creative process. Historically they take their name from the small room where the artwork would traditionally be displayed.

I DID IT: ☐   mfastpete.org/exh/explore-the-vaults-4

DID YOU KNOW?

The MFA's collection has more than 20,000 pieces including major works by the French artists Monet, Morisot, Barye, Rodin, Corot, and Bourdelle, and American artists such as Inness, Hassam, Bellows, O'Keeffe, Pearlstein and Andrew Wyeth. Also on view are ancient Greek and Roman, Egyptian, Asian, African, pre-Columbian, and Native American Art.

GET EDUCATED

ABOUT ESTUARIES

WHAT'S THE DEAL? The Tampa Bay Watch Discovery Center is Tampa Bay Watch's educational space you can visit on the St. Petersburg Pier. The display emphasizes the local fragile ecosystem and Tampa Bay Watch's past and present work to rebuild it.

DO IT IF: You wish to learn about estuaries and aspects of Tampa Bay's abundant waters.

SKIP IT IF: You possess a Ph.D. in marine biology with an emphasis on West Florida eco-systems.

LOCAL ADVICE: Be sure to check out the exhibit gallery featuring native and invasive frogs and toads, learning how you can tell them apart. Also stop by and say hi to Bertha and Ruby, two rare ornate diamondback turtles. If you wish to see the eco-system up close, take one of the daily eco-boat tours, departing directly from the pier.

I DID IT: ☐ www.tbwdiscoverycenter.org

DID YOU KNOW?

Estuaries are called the "nurseries of the sea" because they are breeding grounds, providing protection for newly hatched fish and other marine life to hide and eat like small crabs and turtles. Around Tampa Bay, red mangroves are an essential nursery habitat and provide protection from erosion during strong coastal storms and hurricanes.

37

FIND THE CHILEAN FLAMINGOS

WHAT'S THE DEAL? Sunken Gardens in historic St. Petersburg's Northeast neighborhood, is one of those last great Florida roadside attractions.

DO IT IF: You just love to wander more than a century old garden with mature vegetation.

SKIP IT IF: You only look forward and never want to visit the past.

LOCAL ADVICE: The Sunken Garden is where you can wander rambling paths through a living collection of more than 50,000 tropical plants and flowers with lush gardens featuring cascading waterfalls dating back to 1911. A plumber named George Turner, purchased the six acres and used an elaborate maze of clay tiles, to drain a lake on the property. Neighbors so enjoyed strolling through Mr. Turner's garden, that by the early 1930's he was able nickel for tours, and the sunken gardens was born. And yes, this is where you can find their flock of Chilean Flamingos.

I DID IT: ☐ www.stpete.org/visitors/sunken_gardens.php

DID YOU KNOW?

The sunken gardens flock of flamingos recently became social media darlings during killer hurricane Ian in 2022. A photo of the flock huddled in the garden's bathroom to ride out the storm went worldwide. Good news to report post storm, the flamingos rode out the massive hurricane unscathed!

SHOP AT SUNDIAL

WHAT'S THE DEAL?   Looking for a lively and chic shopping experience in Downtown St. Petersburg? We found it for you at the Sundial Mall.

DO IT IF: You delight in buying your clothes at nationally known retail stores.

SKIP IT IF: You only shop thrift and consignment shops.

LOCAL ADVICE: Shops and Sundial include Tommy Bahama, White House/Black Market and Chico's amongst others. There are also fine dining options like Ruth Chris steakhouse and a multiplex movie theater for a full day of Downtown Fun for everyone.

I DID IT: ☐   sundialstpete.com

DID YOU KNOW?

A shopping complex called Baywalk, originally opened on the location in 2000. The project met with limited financial success. A local businessman bought the property in 2011, and after a multi-million dollar renovation, the newly re-branded complex known as The Mall at Sundial was born.

CLIMB TO THE TOP

WHAT'S THE DEAL? There is an observation tower inside a nature preserve, that once you reach the top, you will have an unforgettable 360-degree view.

DO IT IF: You strive to get to the top.

SKIP IT IF: You are fine with the view from sea level.

LOCAL ADVICE: The Weedon Island preserve offers a total of 4.7 miles of nature trails for hiking with 2 miles out of the total as boardwalks and paved trails that are ADA accessible, and the remaining 2.7 miles as natural trail loops. The 3,000-foot-long tower boardwalk trail leads visitors to the 45-foot tall observation tower, the tallest in Pinellas County. With clear weather conditions, you'll see much of the Preserve and Tampa Bay from this tower, as well as the cities of Tampa and St. Petersburg.

I DID IT: floridahikes.com/weedon-island-preserve

DID YOU KNOW?

In 2011, archaeologists excavated an ancient dugout canoe from the shoreline of Weedon Island Preserve. The makers of the canoe are considered to belong to the Manasota culture, a prehistoric Native American people who hunted and fished the bay, leaving shell mounds along the coast.

BRING ON A BAND

WHAT'S THE DEAL?   Clearwater has a 73,000 square foot performing arts center, which is considered state of the art.

DO IT IF: You relish a musical performance with world class acoustics.

SKIP IT IF: You prefer an outdoor concert venue like you experienced at Woodstock.

LOCAL ADVICE: Ruth Eckerd Hall has hosted world famous bands, musicians, dance companies and even Broadway plays. Noted performers over the years include the B-52's, Paul Anka, Tom Jones and the Monkees. If there is a band or performance you really want to see, book your tickets early, the venue seats just over 2,100 guests.

I DID IT: ☐   www.rutheckerdhall.com

DID YOU KNOW?

The venue opened in 1983 and is a popular performance venue of the Florida Orchestra. The hall features what is known as continental seating, there is no main center aisle. In 2019 the hall underwent a multi-million-dollar re-imagination and is truly first class once again.

FORECAST THE PHILS

WHAT'S THE DEAL? It is a sure sign that summer is coming, the annual migration of baseball players to the gulf coast to prepare for the upcoming season.

DO IT IF: You fancy yourself as an amateur scout, and you know which highly touted rookie or aging veteran will help the team win.

SKIP IT IF: You'll wait until the world series to catch up on your team.

LOCAL ADVICE: The spring training home of the "fighting Phillies" is BayCare Park in Clearwater. It is honestly one of the nicest stadiums in the Grapefruit League, with great sightlines from nearly every seat in the stadium. The stands hold roughly 7,300 fans which sounds like a lot. Keep in mind, especially when the Yankees or Red Sox are in Clearwater for a game, tickets sell out fast. Lots of snowbirds and northern visitors escaping the winter are in town so seats sell out fast!

I DID IT: ☐ www.mlb.com/phillies/spring-training

DID YOU KNOW?

The Phillies have been training in Clearwater, Florida, since 1947, the second-longest affiliation between a major league club and its spring training home in baseball.

TAKE PART IN A 10K

WHAT'S THE DEAL?   There is a popular 10k which offers unforgettable vistas and can only be done one day a year.

DO IT IF: You like to take on a challenge and push yourself in an amazing setting.

SKIP IT IF: What time do the bus shuttles start? 5am?...

LOCAL ADVICE: The annual Skyway bridge run is limited to roughly 8,000 runners so plan ahead. The money raised goes to help local military families, so your pain is their gain. Race participants can park, free of charge at Tropicana field, then walk to the bus pickup location to shuttle you to the starting line. Keep in mind, buses leave early, starting at 5:30am.

I DID IT: ☐   www.skyway10k.com

DID YOU KNOW?

The original bridge Sunshine Skyway Bridge opened for traffic on September 6, 1954. Sadly, in May of 1980, a freighter hit and collapsed a section of the Skyway, causing 35 fatalities. The New Skyway opened in 1987 and at its peak, is 180 feet above Tampa Bay.

JUMP INTO THE
DEEP END

WHAT'S THE DEAL? There is a fun, funky shopping spot in the Grand Central district of St. Petersburg than is worth a visit.

DO IT IF: You enjoy supporting local business that put out a fun vibe.

SKIP IT IF: You're more of a mall or big box store shopper.

LOCAL ADVICE: Artpool's Gallery and Vintage shop has been going strong since 2008. Their forte is vintage clothing, handmade jewelry, antiques and you can even find vinyl record albums here as well. Check out their store calendar for their popular monthly gallery nights as well!

I DID IT: ☐ www.artpoolrules.com

DID YOU KNOW?

You can support a local business, without even leaving home. Artpool offers a mystery giftbox of earrings, necklaces, pins, or rings. Order online and send it to a friend or loved one as a special and thoughtful gift.

SAVOR SPRINKLES

WHAT'S THE DEAL? When you just need some fresh homemade ice cream, near the beach, we have a place for you!

DO IT IF: You live for fresh, homemade frozen treat!

SKIP IT IF: You are watching your figure.

LOCAL ADVICE: Sprinkles in St Pete Beach offers all the traditional flavors, made in small batches to ensure that fresh ice cream flavor. They even have their own creations, like trash can, birthday cake, cookie monster and our personal favorite, Toasted Coconut!

I DID IT: ☐ sprinklesspb.com

DID YOU KNOW?

The range of milk fat used in ice cream can go from around 10 percent to a maximum of about 16 percent. Most premium ice creams use 14 percent milk fat. The higher the fat content the richer the taste and creamier the texture. Sprinkles is considered "Premium" with 14% !

EMBRACE AN ALLIGATOR

WHAT'S THE DEAL?   Believe it or not, there is a wildlife rescue facility that wants you to be hands on, and even smooch a gator!

DO IT IF: You love all of God's creatures.

SKIP IT IF: You just don't trust all those teeth, to get that close.

LOCAL ADVICE: The Alligator and Wildlife Discovery Center in Madeira Beach has a simple mission. They wish to provide humane, professional care for pet surrenders and orphaned native wildlife that cannot be safely returned to the wild. The Center is home to over 250 animals including lizards, small mammals, amphibians, turtles and tortoises, fresh and saltwater marine life, and of course....alligators. Stop by and embrace some local wildlife!

I DID IT: ☐   kissagator.com

DID YOU KNOW?

The Alligator Attraction was founded in 2011 has grown by leaps and bounds to rescue and rehab many different kinds of reptiles and mammals alike. That being said, they updated their name to the Alligator & Wildlife Discovery Center in 2020 and are fully licensed by the USDA, Florida Fish and Wildlife Conservation Commission, Florida Department of Agriculture.

SAMPLE CITRUS WINE

WHAT'S THE DEAL? Wine is basically fermented fruit, right? So why not make it from tasty Florida citrus? Well, there is winery in St Petersburg that agrees.

DO IT IF: You enjoy locally made wines with a citrus flair.

SKIP IT IF: Your A.A. sponsor would certainly frown on you drinking any alcoholic beverage. Or you are under 21 years of age of course.

LOCAL ADVICE: Florida Orange Groves Winery, is a third generation, family owned and operated, tropical fruit winery. It all started out in the 1970's in St. Petersburg. They grew the fruit operation to include retail sales of fresh squeezed juice with an onsite gift shop. They started developing fruit wines over 25 years ago and now are a fully operational working winery.

I DID IT: ☐ floridawine.com

DID YOU KNOW?

The Florida Orange Groves Winery has an onsite tasting room, some stop by and sample some of their most popular vintages. Those wines include Mango Mamma, Orange Blossom Honey, Orange Sunshine Sweet and Key West Limen.

EXPERIENCE 8 GALLERIES OF ART

WHAT'S THE DEAL? If you are excited by Western Art, there is a museum in Downtown St. Petersburg with an extensive collection.

DO IT IF: You can't get enough of Western Art and Sculpture.

SKIP IT IF: Western Art was your mom's uncle who moved to Tucson in the 1980's.

LOCAL ADVICE: The James Museum's art includes paintings, sculpture, jewelry, and artifacts by 20th and 21st century artists, dedicated to Native American and Western themed Art. The collection is strong in contemporary Western paintings, created since 1980 and is well organized into 8 distinctive Galleries for your viewing pleasure.

I DID IT: ☐ thejamesmuseum.org

DID YOU KNOW?

Early artists such as George Catlin, Albert Bierstadt, Thomas Moran, and Frederic Remington became well known for their Western subjects. The works which were widely published back East, creating curiosity, and even enticing pioneers and cowboys to pack up and seek a new life out west.

HAVE AN EPIPHANY

WHAT'S THE DEAL?   There is an annual celebration in Tarpon Spring, were having an Epiphany is expected by all who attend.

DO IT IF: You are seeking an eye-opening experience while learning about a different culture.

SKIP IT IF: You feel like you are already enlightened sufficiently.

LOCAL ADVICE: Tarpon Spring carries on a tradition, brought to the area by sponge divers in the early 1900's. The Archbishop of the Greek Orthodox Church will throw a gold cross in the water and a swarm of young men from the community, feverously dive in to retrieve it. The young man who eventually retrieves it is blessed by the archbishop and is said to possess favorable luck the rest of his days.

I DID IT: ☐   spongedocks.net/tarpon-springs-epiphany

DID YOU KNOW?

The Orthodox Church celebrates Epiphany on January 6th of each year, in remembrance of the baptism of Jesus in the River Jordan. The tradition continues in Tarpon Springs with the blessing of the sponge fleet to protect them from hurricanes and diving for the gold cross.

DANCE AT A
HISTORIC CASINO

WHAT'S THE DEAL? There is a historic casino that is the place to be on Wednesday nights for swing dancing.

DO IT IF: Swing dancing is your passion!

SKIP IT IF: You suffer from Chorophobia.

LOCAL ADVICE: The historic Gulfport Casino, just steps from the water, hosts on of the hottest nights in all of Pinellas County. You don't even need a partner, just turn up and you can be paired up with someone else who also lives for swing dancing. If Argentinian Tango dancing is your style, they have a night for that too, Tuesday!

I DID IT: ☐ www.swingtime.info
mygulfport.us/recreation/casino

DID YOU KNOW?

The Historic Gulfport Casino was built in 1934 and located only a few steps away from Boca Ciega Bay. The architecture and ambiance make the Historic Gulfport Casino one of the most unique ballroom dance venues in the State of Florida.

50

WE'RE GOING ANTIQUING

WHAT'S THE DEAL?   As you can imagine, there are no shortage of antique shop to find that once in a lifetime discovery.

DO IT IF: Your lifelong goal is to find an item so rare, the appraiser on Antiques Roadshow will be in awe.

SKIP IT IF: You only buy stuff from this decade.

LOCAL ADVICE: There are 2 local places, both on Central Avenue in St Petersburg that seem to have all things antiques covered. Lions Paw has an amazing collection of military items, camera equipment, toys, and train sets for sale. Vintage Modern specializes in home good and has a vast selection of vinyl records as well. And good news for collectors, they are always buying and selling, so the inventory changes frequently.

I DID IT: www.lionspawantiquesandjewelry.com
vintage-modern-st-pete.business.site

DID YOU KNOW?

In 2017, the Antique Roadshow's highest-valued item came via two British soldiers, a Faberge flower. The stunning six-inch-tall flower was crafted using gold, silver, enamel and jade with a diamond center and carved rock crystal base. It's one of the only surviving 'botanical studies' created by Faberge in the early 1900s. The valuation, given by the show's Faberge jewelry expert, stood at just over 1 million dollars.

HEAD TO THE "END OF THE ROAD"

WHAT'S THE DEAL? There is a secluded beach, boutique shops, ferries to nearby islands and historic district, literally at the end of the road.

DO IT IF: You like to explore new places, just south of St. Pete Beach.

SKIP IT IF: The beach you are currently sitting at will do just fine, thank you very much.

LOCAL ADVICE: There really is a lot to do at the end of the road here. Waterfront dining, ferries to Shell Key from Merry Pier , fishing excursions, a history museum, paddleboard rentals as well as a nightly sunset celebration tradition.

I DID IT: ☐ www.visitpassagrille.com

DID YOU KNOW?

There is a nightly sunset tradition in Pass-A-Grill beach that is still carried on to this day. Thanks to self-proclaimed head ding dong, Jim LeBlanc and his team of volunteers, a bell is rung for sunset, rain or shine. Come and celebrate this tradition and with family and friends, to create life long memories.

SNORKEL SHELL KEY

WHAT'S THE DEAL? Take the ferry to shell key, to experience some of the best snorkeling in the entire Tampa Bay area.

DO IT IF: You are amazed by the marine eco-system and want to see the fish who live here literally face to face.

SKIP IT IF: You prefer to view marine life from a safe distance or perhaps behind aquarium glass.

LOCAL ADVICE: Shell Key Preserve is a popular sanctuary for nesting, wintering, and migrating birds, as well as a popular fishing and boating area just south of St. Pete Beach. Access to Shell Key is only by private boats or public ferries like the Shell Key Shuttle, there is no bridge to the island. Please pack plenty of water and sunblock when you visit, services are limited once you arrive.

I DID IT: ☐ shellkeyshuttle.com
pinellas.gov/parks/shell-key-preserve

DID YOU KNOW?

Shell Key Preserve in just over 1800 acres of undeveloped mangroves , seagrass beds and beach dunes. The key also provides a nesting area for both local and migrating shorebirds, so Shell Key also offers some great bird watching.

GET ROWDIE

WHAT'S THE DEAL? There is a popular local soccer club that encourages its fans to "Get Rowdie!"

DO IT IF: You marvel at the intricacies of the "beautiful game."

SKIP IT IF: Your sport needs more scoring than nil to nil.

LOCAL ADVICE: The Rowdies have been entertaining local fans since 1975 when they originally played in Tampa Stadium. The current franchise plays its home games in historic Al Lang stadium in downtown St. Petersburg and participates in the USL championship league. Rowdies' games are very well attended by a rabid fan base, who love to "Get Rowdie!"

I DID IT: ☐ www.rowdiessoccer.com

DID YOU KNOW?

The USL Championship was formed when two existing professional leagues were combined into a single league property before the 2011 season. The league was designed to help ensure the long-term stability of professional soccer in North America and games are broadcast across the ESPN family of networks.

CATCH A SHOW AT
THE STATE THEATER

WHAT'S THE DEAL? The old State Theater has been re-imagined into an entertainment venue offering amazing aerial performances.

DO IT IF: Old restored Theatres inspire you to attend, no matter what or who is on stage.

SKIP IT IF: Old restored Theaters frighten you because of possible hauntings.

LOCAL ADVICE: The Floridian Social Club who now operates within this historic building has live entertainment and aerial performances every Friday and Saturday featuring Taylor Roberts, Emily Torres and rotating special performers. They strive to showcase a variety of artistic performances, including aerial acts, contortionists, cabaret, burlesque, and more! Think cirque-de-sole Florida style. There is always a fun vibe, no matter what type of show you catch here!

I DID IT: www.floridiansocialclub.live

DID YOU KNOW?

The building was constructed as Alexander National Bank in 1924.. At that time, the 6,000-square-foot building made it one of the largest banks in St. Petersburg. The Fidelity Bank and Trust Company purchased the building in July 1929. The stock market crash in October forced the bank to close. After Fidelity's liquidation in 1931, the building was used for a succession of small office tenants until 1949 when it was transformed into the State Theatre.

JAM ON A JET SKI

WHAT'S THE DEAL? One of the most exhilarating experiences you can live through on the Gulf of Mexico is going full throttle on a jet ski.

DO IT IF: You are super pumped to glide over the water at 50MPH!

SKIP IT IF: You prefer more carbon friendly boating activities or have had a few drinks. Don't drink and boat!

LOCAL ADVICE: Bind Pass on St. Pete Beach is a good jumping off point for a Jet Ski rental. You will have a large ride area of 5 x 2 miles. If you are hesitant to ride unfamiliar areas on your own, they offer guided tours of the area as well to see places like shell key and Fort DeSoto state park.

I DID IT: ☐ www.blindpassboatandjetski.com/jet-ski-rentals

DID YOU KNOW?

Ride with a reputable company with newer Jet Skis. Blind Pass offers 2019 Sea Doo GTI pro models which can handle 2 riders up to 400 pounds total with tops speeds of 50 Mph. If a company offers you a Sea Doo Spark rental, RUN! They are slow and uncomfortable to ride. That's coming from a former Jet Ski guide in Key West!

ASPIRE TO BE AN ARTIST

WHAT'S THE DEAL? There are numerous places in the Greater St. Peterburg area where you too can take classes in various mediums and become an artist yourself!

DO IT IF: You have always wanted to be a landscape painter but just were not sure how to start.

SKIP IT IF: Painting, drawing, making pottery or even photography are nowhere on your radar.

LOCAL ADVICE: The Dunedin fine arts center has adult art classes for literally artists of all skill levels, even if you have never picked up a paint brush in your life. The Morean art center in St. Petersburg also offers adult art education in various styles including drawing, metal sculpture, photography, glass, clay and more. Sign up fast if you are at all interested, space is limited.

I DID IT: ☐   www.dfac.org/classes
moreanartscenter.org/classes

DID YOU KNOW?

Grandma Moses, was an American folk artist who began painting at the age of 78. French Impressionist Claude Monet didn't begin his painting prowess until his 40's after the passing of his wife. So it's never too late to learn!

RECEIVE THE CELEBRITY TREATMENT

WHAT'S THE DEAL?   As far luxury accommodations go in the Greater St. Petersburg area, there is one place to stay that literally has hosted dozens of celebrities.

DO IT IF: You wish to be treated like a star athlete, Hollywood luminary and or President during your hotel stay.

SKIP IT IF: You are good with self-parking outside your room and a free continental breakfast.

LOCAL ADVICE: The Vinoy Park Hotel was built in 1925 by oil tycoon Aymer Vinoy Laughner. It originally operated as a seasonal hotel, open from around December to March. Rates were $20.00 a night, the highest in the area at that time. The Vinoy was very popular with famous athletes, politicians and famous actors like Babe Ruth, Herbert Hoover, Calvin Coolidge, and Jimmy Stewart. The hotel was vacant for many years before being restored to its original glory in 1990 and is currently on the National Register of Historic places.

I DID IT: ☐   www.marriott.com/en-us/hotels

DID YOU KNOW?

> After a brief stint during WW II as a military housing, the Vinoy regained its prominence as a celebrity hangout. Publicity shy Yankee legend Joe DiMaggio was often caught sneaking into the resort alongside his starlet wife, the actress Marilyn Monroe.

FIND "OLD " FLORIDA

WHAT'S THE DEAL? When you say old history in Florida, you are mostly talking about the late 19th and early 20th century.

DO IT IF: You are thankful many of the earliest building from St Petersburg earliest days still exist.

SKIP IT IF: You have traveled to Europe, now that's old history.

LOCAL ADVICE: You only need to traverse a few blocks of downtown St. Petersburg's to find its earliest construction. Literally along 1st and 2nd Streets and Avenues and of course Central Avenue, is a well-preserved historic district, well worth a visit. Look for the 1909 St. Petersburg Yacht Club, The Ponce De Leon Hotel from 1922 and at 25 2nd street you'll find the Florentine Hotel Building, completed in 1910. The link below has a pretty detailed self-guided walking tour of the area if you want to see it for yourself.

I DID IT: ☐ floridahistory.org/ST-PETERSBURG.htm

DID YOU KNOW?

Even the U.S post office in St. Petersburg is considered historic. It has an open air design with a Mediterranean Revival style building reminiscent of architecture found in early renaissance Florence, Italy. The Post office at 400 N. 1st Avenue opened for business for 1917.

ENJOY A "SWEET TREAT"

WHAT'S THE DEAL? You only live once, so every once in a while, you should treat yourself.

DO IT IF: You have worked hard and deserve a treat, or you have a massive sweet tooth.

SKIP IT IF: You are training for a body building contest, and you must maintain your less than 2 percent body fat.

LOCAL ADVICE: Bruno's Bakery Café has more than 30 years of making sweet treats for all occasions. If you are looking for a cake for a special occasion, need cookies to take to a picnic or just need to satisfy that sweet tooth, with a donut, éclair or Cheesecake, Bruno's has what you need.

I DID IT: ☐   www.facebook.com/brunosbakerycafe

DID YOU KNOW?

It was the Ancient Greeks who adopted the tradition of giving cakes. Well, the Greeks needed something to offer up to Artemis, goddess of the moon, as a tribute on their birthdays. The Greeks baked moon-shaped cakes and adorned them with lit candles so they would shine like the moon.

60

FOLLOW IN THE FOOTSTEPS
OF THE 1ST FLORIDIANS

WHAT'S THE DEAL? There are traces throughout Pinellas County of Native American settlements , if you know where to look.

DO IT IF: You are really intrigued by the Native People who inhabited the area before the 1st Europeans arrived.

SKIP IT IF: You have seen the Native American history exhibit when you walk into the casino.

LOCAL ADVICE: One of the best Native American sites is in Safety Harbor, inside Phillipe Park. The park itself was once part of the 1st grapefruit plantation in Florida. The location is thought to be the center of the Tocobaga Tribe, perhaps the capital of their civilization with a large, high, mounded temple built with shells and sand with a smaller burial mound close by.

I DID IT: ☐   seesafetyharbor.com/Philippe-Park
pinellas.gov/tocobaga-temple-mound

DID YOU KNOW?

The once thriving Tocobaga Tribe, which populated much of the area, had literally disappeared from the map by the early 1700's. They most likely were decimated by disease carried by Spanish explorers in the late 1500 and early 1600's. Sadly some of the survivors were likely captured by the Spaniards and forced to work on Cuban Plantations.

FIND THE FILMING LOCATIONS

WHAT'S THE DEAL? One of my favorite activities is when I visit a city is to seek out famous filming locations and see how the Hollywood lens has perceived it.

DO IT IF: You are a big movie buff and enjoy seeing local locations that have made it on to the "Silver Screen."

SKIP IT IF: You could care less about movies or see where historic movie scenes were actually filmed.

LOCAL ADVICE: Both St. Petersburg and Clearwater have served as the backdrop for numerous Hollywood blockbusters over the years. Some of the more notable movies filmed locally include Ocean's Eleven (2001), Once Upon a Time in America (1984), Miss Peregrine's Home for Peculiar Children (2016), Magic Mike (2012), Spring Breakers (2012), The Punisher (2004), Summer Rental (1985), Cocoon (1985). Test your movie trivia knowledge and find them for yourself!

I DID IT: [ ] www.imdb.com/search/title

DID YOU KNOW?

Early on in Oceans 11, there was a scene shot at the Derby Lane Dog Track. The most iconic movie shot almost entirely in St. Petersburg was Cocoon. Look for the local locations including the St. Petersburg Shuffleboard Club, Suncoast Manor Retirement Community, the Coliseum, and Snell Arcade.

62

HEAD TO HONEYMOON
ISLAND

WHAT'S THE DEAL? If you are looking for a tranquil, unspoiled Island paradise, we have the place for you to visit.

DO IT IF: You enjoy a relaxing day trip without hopping on a plane and flying to the Caribbean.

SKIP IT IF: If you are going to an island, you are flying to St. Marteen.

LOCAL ADVICE: Another one of the St. Petersburg and Clearwater area State Parks in Honeymoon Island, just off the coast of Dunedin. Before a Hurricane in 1921, Honeymoon Island and Caladesi Island were one large landmass known as Hog Island. The hurricane split the island in 2 and created Hurricane Pass. With 4 miles of white sandy beaches, walking trails, bird watching and even an untouched pine forest and unforgettable sunset. Take the trip and see why, this is one of the area's most popular State Parks.

I DID IT: ☐   www.floridastateparks.org/honeymoonisland

DID YOU KNOW?

In the late 1930s, a businessman named Clinton Washburn purchased the island. While having lunch with a friend who was the editor of Life magazine, he made a comment that the island would make a wonderful site for honeymoons. Life magazine published the story and Honeymoon Island was born.

FLY TO PIE

WHAT'S THE DEAL? For a no hassle visit to St. Petersburg, avoid that big international airport across the bay, and fly directly into PIE!

DO IT IF: You want to hit the beach ASAP instead of waiting for your luggage coming off the conveyer belt.

SKIP IT IF: Your airmiles only allow you to fly into crowded big city airports.

LOCAL ADVICE: St. Peterburg/Clearwater International airport offers more than 60 direct flights, with convenient parking a short walk from the gates. Allegiant Air offers the most flights from smaller Northeast, Southeast and Midwest Airports offering you an inexpensive way to get away. Sun Country also offers non-stop flights from Minneapolis. If you have a small group of interested students, PIE even offers educational tours to get behind the scenes.

I DID IT: ☐ fly2pie.com

DID YOU KNOW?

After the Japanese attack on Pearl Harbor in 1941, the airfield was constructed to train P-40 and P-51 pilots. After the war, the airfield was donated to the county and gained the name, Pinellas International Airport, PIE!

64

MAKE TIME FOR
TRAIN WEEKEND

WHAT'S THE DEAL? There is a monthly event, that brings train enthusiasts of all ages from near and far to a Largo Park.

DO IT IF: You are a model train enthusiast or are liking for a fun, free activity for the family.

SKIP IT IF: You rode the train to work for 35 years, your riding the train days are over!

LOCAL ADVICE: Enjoy a ride around beautiful Largo Central Park on their miniature railroad on the first full weekend of the month from 10am-4pm. The precisely modeled scale locomotives pull you and your family along a mile-long loop through great scenery, a spooky tunnel, and past a waterfall pond. It is a blast for all ages. There is no charge for this family-fun activity, but donations are certainly welcome because your generosity keep the trains running.

I DID IT: ☐   www.playlargo.com/special_event_detail_T38_R13.php
lcrailroad.org

DID YOU KNOW?

The Largo Central Railroad is run by a dedicated group of volunteers of all ages, who share one thing in common. They love railroads and it shows in the intricacy of the trains they operate. They feature steam engines, just like the originals, modern Diesel Locomotives and very detailed passenger cars.

BE ONE WITH
BUTTERFLIES

WHAT'S THE DEAL? Head up the road to Dunedin to marvel at one of nature's most versatile yet fragile creatures.

DO IT IF: You marvel at the beauty of Butterflies especially when you see them up close.

SKIP IT IF: The thought of butterflies floating around you, freaks you out or you suffer from Lepidopterophobia.

LOCAL ADVICE: Head to Hammock Park for their amazing butterfly garden, the perfect place to watch natural beauty take flight. The garden was created for the entire community to enjoy with 225 plants in 40 different varieties. Follow the crushed shell pathway which takes visitors through an extraordinary flower display with numerous butterfly favorites. Hidden away on a quiet street, local treasure Hammock Park, is home to more than 35 species of butterflies.

I DID IT: ☐ hammockpark.org/butterfly

DID YOU KNOW?

The Monarch and Tiger Swallowtail are 2 of the species you are likely to encounter at Hammock Park. Although it is hard to imagine, every autumn, the seemingly fragile Monarch Butterflies migrate over 3,000 miles from the Northeast to their breeding grounds in Mexico.

ANGLE INSHORE

WHAT'S THE DEAL? If you are a fishing fanatic, hit the shallows to battle some of Florida's most ferocious game fish.

DO IT IF: You enjoy the chess match between you and your elusive prize.

SKIP IT IF: You only travel miles offshore to try to hook a sailfish or shark.

LOCAL ADVICE: Fishing inshore or on the flats requires an experienced guide who know the inlets, mangroves, bayous, and sandbars at high and low tides. Here you will encounter some of the most prized game fish like snook, grouper and both black and red drum.

I DID IT: ☐ clearwaterflatsfishing.com

DID YOU KNOW?

There are more than 400 different species of grouper but the most popular are Black and Red Grouper. This type of fish has a very mild flavor, with a light, sweet taste and large, chunky flakes, almost like lobster or crab. Enjoy it deep fried on a sandwich or blackened will all the fixings.

COMMEMORATE AFRICAN AMERICAN HISTORY

WHAT'S THE DEAL? Learn about some of the early and influential African Americans who blazed a trail making St Peterburg one of the most diverse in the South.

DO IT IF: You appreciate knowing about all races, creeds and colors who came before you.

SKIP IT IF: You are more interested in happy hour or fishing.

LOCAL ADVICE: There is a wonderful museum, highlighting the contributions African Americans made in the development of St. Petersburg. The first African Americans came to this area seeking work. Many of the early migrants worked on the Orange Belt Railroad and other early enterprises. As St. Petersburg grew into a major tourist mecca, more jobs were available these early residents.

I DID IT: ☐ woodsonmuseum.org

DID YOU KNOW?

The museum is named for Dr. Carter G. Woodson an early pioneer for African American rights. He attended University of Chicago and received a Ph.D. in history from Harvard in 1912. His claim to fame was naming February "Black History" month to celebrate the birthdays of both Abraham Lincoln and Frederick Douglass.

TRAVEL BY TROLLEY

WHAT'S THE DEAL? Downtown St. Petersburg has a free trolley shuttle service, to get you around, especially with parking being a challenge. Keep in mind, only the downtown looper is free of charge, the other trolley lines collect a fare.

DO IT IF: You want the hassle-free option of not having to worry about parking and leave the driving to a local expert.

SKIP IT IF: Your car goes everywhere with you.

LOCAL ADVICE: Look for the downtown looper, to take you hassle free to most of the downtown attractions, hotels, and museums with complimentary narration from many of the friendly and experienced drivers. These professionals have the patience of saints, not only to deal with the general public but also the sometimes chaotic downtown St. Petersburg traffic. Any gratuity you wish to share with them is appreciated, trust me they earn it!

I DID IT: ☐ www.psta.net/riding-psta/schedulesmap/ downtown-looper/

DID YOU KNOW?

St. Petersburg once had an electric trolley system, starting in 1905. Many of the lines would take riders to The Million Dollar Pier. Officially opening on Thanksgiving Day 1926, it featured a swimming area (Spa Beach), solarium and bathhouse. A casino was built as well, where visitors could enjoy dancing and gambling. The casino had a central atrium where streetcars were loaded and unloaded.

PAY A VISIT
TO PIER 60

WHAT'S THE DEAL? Visit Clearwater to find a more than 1000-foot pier extending into the Gulf of Mexico with all kinds of fun things to do.

DO IT IF: You really like being out and over the water.

SKIP IT IF: Walking over the water makes you uneasy.

LOCAL ADVICE: Pier 60 features a well-stocked bait shop and is very popular for night fishing, with numerous lights that attract the fish. There is an abundance of Spanish mackerel, snook, redfish, sheepshead, and snappers. There is also a fabulous sunset celebration and a spectacular sandcastle competition, making this a can't miss destination. Don't worry, if you didn't pack your fishing gear, the onsite bait shop will rent you some.

I DID IT: ☐ www.sunsetsatpier60.com

DID YOU KNOW?

For over 27 years, Pier 60 has been celebrating those fabulous Gulf Coast painted skies at the end of each day. Sunsets at Pier 60 on Clearwater Beach operate year-round from two hours before and after sunset, weather permitting. The nightly celebration features artisans, street performers and the true star, Pier 60 sunsets, which rarely disappoint.

70

MAKE YOUR WAY
TO MAZZARO'S

WHAT'S THE DEAL? If you have relocated from the Northeast and miss true Italian food like you had in the old neighborhood or are just visiting and need your pasta fix, we have the place for you.

DO IT IF: You are craving Capicola, Mortadella, Provolone and Prosciutto all served on fresh baked Italian bread, Manga!

SKIP IT IF: You have no idea what any of those things are, so fuhgettaboutit.

LOCAL ADVICE: Honestly, this place is amazing, you will think you are in an Italian Market on Federal Hill in Providence or Arthur Avenue in the Bronx. Besides their traditionally deli selections you'll find homemade pastas and raviolis, fresh bread, Italian pasties like cannoli's, rum cake and even gelato. They even have an extensive beer and wine selection so stop by and reminisce about the old neighborhood, Benvenuto!

I DID IT: ☐ www.mazzarosmarket.com

DID YOU KNOW?

Originally from Pittsburgh, husband-and-wife team Sam and Pat Cuccaro opened a coffee roasting operation in St. Petersburg in 1982. 10 years later, they moved to Mazzaro's Italian Market's current location and added a brick oven to bake bread and expanded the Italian market, which feels its been there a hundred years. May it last 100 more! Cent 'Anni

71

SEEK OUT S.H.A.M.C.

WHAT'S THE DEAL? If you dream of a place where anyone regardless of your age can celebrate whimsical art in all forms, we found it.

DO IT IF: Art is a joy in all forms and should be rejoiced in, no matter your age.

SKIP IT IF: You only view the master works of already established, world renowned artists.

LOCAL ADVICE: Safety Harbor Art and Music center has a simple motto: To promote knowledge of and education in the fine arts, the visual arts, and the performing arts. They have certainly achieved if not surpassed their goal. You can find regional musical acts, locally produced artwork, classes in many different mediums and even a tour of "Whimzeyland."

I DID IT: ☐ www.safetyharborartandmusiccenter.com

DID YOU KNOW?

WhimzeyLand is and has been a work in progress for over 30 years and was created by artists Todd Ramquist and Kiaralinda- the Founders of the Safety Harbor Art and Music Center. It is uniquely decorated and even offers rooms to rent if you are seeking out a creative place to stay.

72

DON'T MISS THE
MORNING MARKET

WHAT'S THE DEAL? Part farmers market, part food truck festival, part music festival = 100 % good time!

DO IT IF: Supporting local farms, vendors, musicians, and artists is high on the priority list. And all in one convenient location!

SKIP IT IF: You prefer to spend your money with large corporate entities and international conglomerates or don't do well with crowds.

LOCAL ADVICE: The morning market is held most Saturdays October through May at historic Al Lang Stadium in downtown St. Petersburg. Their smaller Summer Market changes venues for shade. It takes place in Williams Park from June to August. The event is super popular, with roughly 10,000 people not missing the morning market.

I DID IT: ☐ saturdaymorningmarket.com

DID YOU KNOW?

The morning market has been operating since 2002 and is proud to feature local farmers who produce organic and sustainable fruits, vegetables, and meat. Food vendors also offer more than a dozen foods from around the world so come and try something new!

SEARCH FOR THE BEST BBQ

WHAT'S THE DEAL? Technically, Florida is in the south, a region certainly famous for its succulent BBQ.

DO IT IF: You enjoy finding local BBQ spots that take pride in their work, while not breaking the bank.

SKIP IT IF: You only fine dine, with the white tablecloth and all the fancy accoutrements.

LOCAL ADVICE: There are a couple local spots we have found over the years offer authentic smoked BBQ, with great sides, served in a casual setting. Poppa's in Clearwater is no frills and some of the best pulled pork around. We were also wowed by the smoked pig wings at Ozona Pig in Palm Harbor. Who knew pigs could fly?

I DID IT: ☐   www.poppasbarbque.com
theozonapig.com

DID YOU KNOW?

Southern BBQ is so much more than just cooking meat outdoors on an open flame. While regional styles vary, all Southern BBQ involves cooking meat low and slow over an indirect heat. This creates that distinctive smoky taste for which BBQ is known. MMM!

74

BRING YOUR
BINOCULARS

WHAT'S THE DEAL? If you are looking for a great bird watching area, travel to Seminole and enjoy this amazing coastal park.

DO IT IF: Bird watching with or without binoculars is one of your true passions.

SKIP IT IF: The only bird watching you do involve your favorite sports team mascots.

LOCAL ADVICE: Boca Ciega Millennial Park offers 186 acres along the bay. The park is accessible if you are already riding the Pinellas Bike Trail. Besides coastal walking paths, there is a great observation tower, and the recreational area is part of the Great Florida Birding Trail. You also have a boat ramp here to launch a kayak and paddle around tranquil Boca Ciega Bay.

I DID IT: ☐ pinellas.gov/parks/boca-ciega-millennium-park

DID YOU KNOW?

Over 175 different species of birds have been spotted in this Pinellas County park. Look for shore birds like White Ibis, Roseate Spoonbills and Blue Heron. You may also encounter the ubiquitous Brown Pelican and pileated woodpeckers. If you are lucky, you may see a playful river otter, swimming past as well.

75

JUDGE THE
(BLUE) JAYS

WHAT'S THE DEAL? Come and see the snowbird visiting team from North of the Border as they prepare for the upcoming season.

DO IT IF: The Blue Jays are your team, or you enjoy viewing the new seasons teams come into focus.

SKIP IT IF: The pace of baseball is a bit to slow for your short attention span.

LOCAL ADVICE: It's an annual rite of passage with unbridled optimism and hope that this is your team's season will finally win it all. At this point, in spring training, every team is in first place.

I DID IT: ☐ www.mlb.com/bluejays/spring-training

DID YOU KNOW?

Since our friends from the north, The Toronto Blue Jays, became a MLB franchise in 1977, they have only trained in Dunedin, Florida. Originally playing at historic Grant Field, games are now played at the recently renovated TD Ballpark.

76

CELEBRATE THE HOLIDAYS
FLORIDA STYLE

WHAT'S THE DEAL? For all the transplants or seasonal visitors who miss those snowy scenes from back home, Florida does it's best to celebrate the holiday season.

DO IT IF: Celebrating the Christmas or Hannukah season is traditional and want to carry on those traditions as best you can.

SKIP IT IF: Bah Humbug! You left the cold and snow behind and are fine with some colored lights on a Palm Tree.

LOCAL ADVICE: St Petersburg certainly gets in the Holiday Spirit with tree lightings, visits with Santa at local parks and even sledding on man-made snow. Many of the local downtown parks will have extensive light displays and you can even have a snowball fight with elves, to burn off some holiday stress.

I DID IT: ☐   www.stpeteparksrec.org/holidayevents

DID YOU KNOW?

One of the most popular holiday activities, is the annual lighted boat parade, held just offshore from the Vinoy Boat basin. Bring your chairs and delights in the holiday lights, as dozens of decorated boats sail by in the oldest and largest boat parade in all of Tampa Bay.

77

JOIN A PARADE

WHAT'S THE DEAL? St. Petersburg is a festive place and residents don't need much of a reason to celebrate with a variety of parades.

DO IT IF: You embrace the local community and love to participate in a street party any chance you get.

SKIP IT IF: People describe your personality as reclusive or Hermitesq.

LOCAL ADVICE: No matter what time of year you visit or are a year-round resident, St. Petersburg has a parade for that event. There is a very popular parade to celebrate MLK day and one of the region's largest Pride Parades held annually in June. Gulfport has one of the largest 4th of July parades in Pinellas County with fireworks display to follow, of course.

I DID IT: ☐ www.stpete.org/visitors/attractions/major_events.php

DID YOU KNOW?

Mardi Gras is usually synonymous with New Orleans, but St. Petersburg also has a similar event. With all things green, gold, and brown, revel with the extravagant Mardi Gras Parades, complete with elaborate floats and a mass of people at the street parties in St. Petersburg. What you do to collect bead is a personal choice, we won't judge.

78

MARVEL AT CHIHULY'S
GLASS WORKS

WHAT'S THE DEAL? A St. Petersburg Museum has an entire collection dedicated to the pioneering work of glass artist Dale Chihuly.

DO IT IF: You are fascinated how artists can create visually appealing art with vibrant colors from glass.

SKIP IT IF: Glass isn't an art form, it's the vessel from which you consume your adult beverage of choice.

LOCAL ADVICE: The Morean Art Center is truly a world class art museum, and luckily it is located for you to visit in downtown. The permanent collection of glass artwork pioneer Dale Chihuly is one of a kind with the building literally designed to highlight his amazing creations. Chihuly even designed the signature Ruby Red Icicle Chandelier, specifically for the gallery.

I DID IT: ☐ moreanartscenter.org/chihuly-collection-location

DID YOU KNOW?

Dale Chihuly's career was marked by 2 serious accidents, that shaped his path. A car accident in England in 1976, he was blinded in 1 eye. He still continued to blow glass, until 1979 when he dislocated his shoulder body surfing and could no longer hold the pipe. At that point he stepped back for a different view and was able to create as an instructor, with the help of others.

79

BRING ON ALL
DAY BREAKFAST

WHAT'S THE DEAL? Look for the giant humpty-dumpty, next to the rooster statue to get your all-day breakfast fix.

DO IT IF: You wake up at noon and are craving banana chocolate chip pancakes.

SKIP IT IF: To you breakfast is the least important meal of the day.

LOCAL ADVICE: Serving all-day breakfast in a no frills setting, since 1976, is what Skyway Jack's is locally famous for. The close proximity to the Eckerd College campus makes it a must stop, not just college students, but anyone who enjoys a no-frill breakfast. Please keep in mind, no-frills also means not modern nor fancy. The food is the star, not the ambiance.

I DID IT: ☐ www.allmenus.com/fl/saint-petersburg/
508960-skyway-jacks/menu/

DID YOU KNOW?

Skyway Jack was a navy cook, whose wife has now carried on his popular cooking style. Skyway Jacks received a bit of national attention when the Food Network featured the Scrapple dish — a mix of pork hearts, liver and... BRAINS, as the best breakfast dish in Florida. (We have not tried it yet)

PAY YOUR RESPECTS
WITH A VIEW

WHAT'S THE DEAL? If you go to the south side of St. Petersburg, you will find a historic park which pays tributes to local war veterans.

DO IT IF: You appreciate the sacrifices Veterans made for us with the bonus views in a bayside park.

SKIP IT IF: We honestly can't think of good reason not to visit.

LOCAL ADVICE: This is a small tranquil green space of roughly 112 acres, honoring all 5 branches of the armed service with flags and plaques. You will also notice Battlefield Cross, a Sundial, and an Authentic WW II Army Tank. There are also walking trails, a boat launch into Boca Ciega Bay and it is dog friendly. It's a great little spot to relax and reflect about our freedoms thank to Veterans.

I DID IT: ☐ pinellas.gov/parks/war-veterans-memorial-park

DID YOU KNOW?

St. Petersburg played an active role during WWII. The coast guard was kept busy with anti-submarine patrols and the Navy and Army Air Corp used the area for training. After the war many of the soldiers and sailors either returned to vacation or retired to spend their golden years in "The Sunshine City."

ATTEND A
"PORCH PARTY"

WHAT'S THE DEAL? If you are friendly, outgoing and enjoy meeting new people, we have the event for you.

DO IT IF: You are a social creature and enjoy chatting up you neighbors.

SKIP IT IF: You are an introvert or suffer from anthropophobia.

LOCAL ADVICE: A great local event, where residents are proud of their historic neighborhood, Roser Park, combines music, local businesses, and tours of 1920's architecture, it's a can't miss annual experience.

I DID IT: ☐ ilovetheburg.com/roser-park-porchfest-st-pete

DID YOU KNOW?

Pride in ownership is evident in this tree-lined neighborhood, Historic Roser Park. It combines varying architectural styles, with Craftsman bungalows, Colonial Revival and even Prairie homes. You will also encounter 19th-century Greenwood Cemetery, with monuments to Civil War soldiers as well as graves of early pioneers.

SOAR OVER THE SKYWAY

WHAT'S THE DEAL? For an amazing experience, there is one way to get a true "Birds Eye" view of the impressive and iconic Sunshine Skyway Bridge.

DO IT IF: You only live once and want to experience once in a lifetime adventures.

SKIP IT IF: You can see the bridge just fine from Tierra Verde, thank you very much.

LOCAL ADVICE: Executive Helicopter offers multiple tours around St. Petersburg and Clearwater. For a truly unforgettable experience, Soar like a bird, over the Skyway Bridge, especially at sunset. Keep in mind, all tours are a two-person minimum, three-person maximum and their weight cannot exceed 300lbs per seat. Tours depart from the convenient Albert Whitted Airport in downtown St. Petersburg.

I DID IT: ☐   www.833flyheli.com

DID YOU KNOW?

The Sunshine Skyway Bridge is a cable-stayed concrete span that extends over four miles across the mouth of Tampa Bay from St. Petersburg to Bradenton, Florida. A major lifeline for the area, the bridge carries an estimated 50,000 cars and trucks, every day.

SALUTE SUNSET WITH

LIVE MUSIC

WHAT'S THE DEAL? Is there a better way, to appreciate the extraordinary gulf coast sunsets, than with live local, lively bands?

DO IT IF: Live music and live sunsets are a winning combination.

SKIP IT IF: You prefer a peaceful backdrop while watching the sun melt below the horizon.

LOCAL ADVICE: Behind the Beachcomber Resort on St. Pete Beach, is a place with live music 365 days a year. With cold beer, unobstructed sunsets, good food and lively company, life is good at Jimmy B's .

I DID IT: ☐ www.beachcomberflorida.com/jimmy_b_st_pete_beach/

DID YOU KNOW?

The Beachcomber, located just steps from the sand at St. Pete Beach, has been delighting visitors since 1949. With gulf front accommodations, 3 tiki bars and affordable dining options, The Beachcomber is another option for those seeking a hassle-free vacation.

BECOME THE MASTER
OF THE MAINSAIL

WHAT'S THE DEAL? Have you always wanted to learn the finer points of sailing your own sloop? The tranquil, well protected bays around St. Petersburg offer sailors of every skill level an almost perfect location to learn.

DO IT IF: You long to be the captain of your own sailing vessel, gliding over the bay at the whims of the winds.

SKIP IT IF: You are a powerboat guy or gal, the more outboards the better.

LOCAL ADVICE: The St. Petersburg Sailing Center, which can trace its origin all the way to the 1940s, offers opportunities to get aboard one of its boats used to instruct and learn how young and old can get into the hobby of sailing. Kids can start their lifetime of sailing as young as five years old. Their wide range of sailboats and programs make sailing accessible to everyone, no matter your level of experience.

I DID IT: ☐ sailstpete.org, www.sailingworld.com/regatta-series-st-petersburg

DID YOU KNOW?

For seasoned sailing enthusiasts and novices alike, The storied St. Petersburg Yacht Club hosts numerous regattas throughout the year. One of the most popular events on the sailing calendar is the Helly Hansen sailing world regatta.

APPRECIATE ART
DECO ARCHITECTURE

WHAT'S THE DEAL? St. Petersburg had a building boom in the early 20th century, and for architecture buffs, many of the early structures survive to this day.

DO IT IF: You appreciate different architectural styles and the work of 20th century designers and the numerous, yet unnamed construction workers, who made these blueprints a reality.

SKIP IT IF: Art Deco and any other style of architecture does nothing for you.

LOCAL ADVICE: St. Petersburg downtown district boasts one the best-preserved Art Deco and Beaux Arts buildings still standing, Miami Beach not withstanding of course. Of course, the most famous is the Pink Palace, the beach front Don Cesar Hotel. Also look for the first Publix supermarket in St. Petersburg, 16th Street North. just north of Woodlawn Park, now a Family Dollar store. For Beaux Arts style, head to 405 Central Avenue where you will find the impressive Snell Arcade, 1926.

I DID IT: www.stpete.org/business/planning__zoning/historic_
                     preservation.php

DID YOU KNOW?

Art Deco buildings have a sleek, linear appearance with stylized, often geometric ornamentation. The primary façade of Art Deco buildings often feature a series of setbacks that create a stepped outline. Low-relief decorative panels can be found at entrances, around windows, along roof edges and was popular between 1925 and 1940.

87

SEEK SOME SHADE

WHAT'S THE DEAL? If you have been wandering around downtown, checking off all those items from your St. Petersburg bucket list, we have a shady spot to rest for a moment.

DO IT IF: You need to take a break, put your feet up, catch your breath and relax for a moment.

SKIP IT IF: No need for a break, your visit is short, and need to cross the rest of the items off your list.

LOCAL ADVICE: The first thing you will notice when you arrive in North Straub Park, are the large mature Banyan Trees and colorful flowers. The park is relatively small at just under 5 acres but commands a great location for bay and pier views or just relax and watch the boats sail by. A special thanks to the Waterfront Parks Foundation for all the flower beds they have planted, not only here, but throughout the city.

I DID IT: ☐   www.stpeteparksrec.org/northstraubpark

DID YOU KNOW?

St. Petersburg's founding fathers are well represented in the names of prominent locations and parks throughout downtown. The city's cofounders, both lent their names to downtown parks: Demen's Landing Park and Williams Park. Straub Park is named after William L. Straub, who purchased the St. Petersburg Times in 1901 and served as its editor or associate editor for 38 years.

MAKE FRIENDS
WITH A MANATEE

WHAT'S THE DEAL? The primitive, yet mammoth mammal, the manatee, is truly an amazing creature best seen in its natural habitat.

DO IT IF: Mother Nature's creations both great and small, are truly worth seeking out to see in person. In the case of the "Sea Cow" it is definitely not small.

SKIP IT IF: Land cows are really more your type, although they are fairly hard to find in Pinellas County.

LOCAL ADVICE: Nestled neatly between the historic Old Northeast neighborhood and Snell Island to the Northeast is a narrow, curved waterway called Coffee Pot Bayou. There is a great pathway to walk along the water as well where you will encounter the manatees, sometimes with little ones in tow. (In a manner of speaking, Manatee calves are not really little.)

I DID IT: ☐ www.google.com/maps/place/Coffeepot+Bayou
www.savethemanatee.org/manatees

DID YOU KNOW?

Florida manatees are bulky, aquatic mammals and are native to Florida. Adult manatees are typically 9-10 feet long from snout to tail and weigh around 1,000 pounds; however, in rare cases can grow to over 13 feet long and weigh more than 3,500 pounds.

CAMP UNDER THE STARS

WHAT'S THE DEAL? If you are one of those people who want to be one with nature and sleep in a tent under the stars, there are state parks the St. Petersburg area that have you covered.

DO IT IF: A perfect night out includes a sleeping bag, tent and gazing up at a star lit sky.

SKIP IT IF: You would never stay anywhere without a valet, king size bed, turn down service with a chocolate on your pillow and 24-hour room service.

LOCAL ADVICE: Fort De Soto state park is hands down the spot for the true camping under the stars destination for those who want to rough it. Reservations are required for one of the 236 sites, with 14 nights maximum and yes, they fill up quickly! If you are visiting the area, and need more time and a traditional RV park, there is also a KOA site in Madeira Beach.

I DID IT: ☐ pinellas.gov/camping-information/
koa.com/campgrounds/st-petersburg/

DID YOU KNOW?

One of the unexpected benefits of the coronavirus pandemic in 2020 was people reconnecting with the simpler things in life, like camping. Outdoor recreation like camping, hiking, biking, boating, fishing, wildlife watching and finding an isolated beach was social distancing before we knew that term.

ESCAPE REALITY

WHAT'S THE DEAL?   This may be easier for some than others, metaphorically but there is a place where everyone can go and literally Escape Reality!

DO IT IF: You wish to encounter nirvana, leave all your troubles behind and be free, at least for a little while.

SKIP IT IF: No thank you, you are perfectly fine with staying in reality and all the worries and pressures that accompany it.

LOCAL ADVICE: What happens when 60 plus artists are turned loose and create their own art infused with technology wonderland? You get Fairgrounds St. Pete, a fully immersive experience with interactive story driven instillations. In other words, you must see what they have created to believe it. For a visual, think of a modern-day world's fair with 21st century technology.

I DID IT: ☐ fairgrounds.art

DID YOU KNOW?

The Fairground was the brainchild of local business woman and art lover Liz Dimmit. Dimmitt is drawing inspiration from Meow Wolf, an arts and entertainment group based in Santa Fe, New Mexico, and has raised more than a million dollars to launch the full immersion art experience.

90

ENJOY HAPPY HOUR
WITH A HISTORIAN

WHAT'S THE DEAL? If you perhaps find local history a tad dull, spice it up with a drink or two.

DO IT IF: Learning local history and knowing more about your community surroundings is your passion.

SKIP IT IF: Your motto is you never drink and learn.

LOCAL ADVICE: The St. Petersburg Museum of History hosts a popular event called Happy Hour with a Historian. Local experts and authors across a wide variety of topics including Pirates, The Supernatural, saving endangered Florida wildlife and even baseball are covered in these lively symposiums. There is an admission fee and sorry, a cash bar, drinks are not included.

I DID IT: spmoh.com/2021-happy-hour-with-the-historian

DID YOU KNOW?

The St. Petersburg Museum of History is dedicated to covering and preserving the area's diverse and extensive history since its founding in 1920. The city of St. Petersburg gifted the museum site after the 1921 Tampa Bay hurricane destroyed the aquarium that previously sat on the property.

RISE UP FOR REGGAE

WHAT'S THE DEAL? Downtown St. Petersburg hosts an annual festival for fans of Reggae, where literally thousands descend on the city to jam to the tunes.

DO IT IF: You can't help but dance when you hear Reggae music or must see any musical group that contains a "Marley."

SKIP IT IF: You may be sensitive to burning cannabis and the accompanying plumes of smoke that are associated with it.

LOCAL ADVICE: This 3-day outdoor concert and festival at the waterside Vinoy Park is extremely popular, so reserve your hotel rooms and event tickets early. Up to 15,000 reggae revelers have been known to attend daily! Popular performers like Dirty Head, Wiz Khalifa and members of the Marley family are commonly seen performing here as well.

I DID IT: ☐   https://reggaeriseup.com/florida/

DID YOU KNOW?

Reggae Rise Up is an annual event that began as a one-day event in Tampa, Florida in 2015. It was so popular, it was moved to the larger and current location at Vinoy Park in 2016. The festival increased in size from a two-day and three-day weekend event to a four day celebration with up to 15,000 fans in attendance.

92

DINE BEHIND
HISTORIC DOORS

WHAT'S THE DEAL? If you are looking for some great comfort food or a famous grouper sandwich, travel down 4th Street in St. Petersburg and look for the historic doors.

DO IT IF: You enjoy a casual dining experience, with some historic décor and a comfortable, friendly atmosphere.

SKIP IT IF: Your idea of dining out includes, a stuffy Maître D, a tuxedo wearing waiter with caviar and champagne on the menu.

LOCAL ADVICE: The nostalgia is palatable when you walk through the historic doors at Harvey's 4th Street Grill, which has been serving visitors and locals alike since 1984. Try their grouper sandwich, they have proudly served more than 2 million over the years!

I DID IT: ☐ harveys4thstreet.com

DID YOU KNOW?

Have you ever wondered where fixtures and other items go when a historic hotel or property is demolished goes? Much of it can be found here with their doors from the historic Sunshine School in St. Pete Beach.

93

SEE A SEA TURTLE HATCH

WHAT'S THE DEAL? All along the gulf coast every year, the cycle of life plays out along numerous sandy beaches in the area.

DO IT IF: The wonders of nature never cease to amaze you.

SKIP IT IF: You prefer to watch the nature programs on the Discovery channel from the comfort of your Lazy Boy recliner.

LOCAL ADVICE: There is a small island just south of Clearwater Beach, called Sand Key, you can go in person and watch the sea turtles hatch and make their way to the water. Typically, the hatches occur between August and October, with potentially dozens of the little guys frantically scurrying toward the safety of the Gulf of Mexico.

I DID IT: ☐ pinellas.gov/parks/sand-key-park

DID YOU KNOW?

Numerous Gulf Coast beaches are nesting sites to loggerheads, green sea turtles, and the critically endangered Kemp's Ridley sea turtle. The mother always returns to lay eggs at the beach where she hatched. Local marine protection groups will rope off the turtle nest so they are not disturbed and all sea turtles and their eggs are federally protected so DON'T TOUCH!

JAM OUT AT JANNUS

WHAT'S THE DEAL?   If you can't get enough live music, St. Petersburg has got you covered, with an outdoor concert venue that has a historic significance.

DO IT IF: You live for live music, served in a historic venue.

SKIP IT IF: You can't stand to stand for an entire show. Jannus Live is a standing room only venue.

LOCAL ADVICE: Jannis Live in Downtown St. Petersburg is an outdoor concert venue where the mix of old and new come together. The venue features a mix of popular local bands, DJ's and even host private events. If there is a show you are dying to see in person, book early because the capacity at Jannus Live is 2,000 guests and remember, no seating. Standing room only!

I DID IT: ☐   www.jannuslive.com

DID YOU KNOW?

In a tribute to St. Petersburg colorful past, Jannus Live is named in honor of a famous local aviator named Tony Jannus. He was considered the first commercial airline pilot with his flights from St. Petersburg across the bay to Tampa in 1914 on his flying boat biplane.

PICK A PUMPKIN

WHAT'S THE DEAL?   No matter what your Halloween Holiday tradition entails, the greater St. Petersburg area has a plethora of Halloween activities.

DO IT IF: Halloween is your favorite holiday of the year!

SKIP IT IF: You aren't big into dressing up in costumes and are waiting for the Thanksgiving feast.

LOCAL ADVICE: The largest local event takes place on St. Petersburg's Central Avenue with 22 blocks closed to vehicular traffic. There are events, entertainment, parties and costume contests for kids and adults alike, all along the avenue. If your Halloween traditions include picking your own pumpkin, Gallaghers Farm in St. Petersburg grows the colorful gourds for your perusal and hopefully, selection.

I DID IT: ☐   halloweenoncentral2.com
www.gallagherspumpkinsandchristmastrees.com

DID YOU KNOW?

Halloween ranks 2nd only behind Xmas in holiday spending. The National Retail Federation annual estimate projects that spending on Halloween candy, costumes and decorations will hit an all-time high of $10.6 billion in 2022. That's a lot of candy!

EXPERIENCE OMAKASE

WHAT'S THE DEAL? For a true once in a lifetime dining experience, try Omakase.

DO IT IF: You savor fresh fish and sushi, and truly wish to place your dining in the hands of the Chef.

SKIP IT IF: You don't like surprises especially when it comes to raw fish.

LOCAL ADVICE: Sushi Sho Rexley is now offering this unique dining experience where every course is served with a purpose, presentation, and style with fish from all over the world. The courses are also paired with Saki to enhance the overall dining experience. Reservations are required and let them know ahead of time of any dining restrictions, especially if you do not want any surprises.

I DID IT: ☐   www.rexleysushi.com

DID YOU KNOW?

Few formal dining experiences are as revered or as intimidating as omakase, a form of Japanese dining in which guests leave themselves in the hands of a chef and receive a meal which is seasonal, elegant, artistic and uses the finest ingredients available. Literally translated it means, "I Leave it up to you."

REMEMBERING "WORLD'S MOST UNUSUAL DRUG STORE"

WHAT'S THE DEAL? St. Petersburg was once the home to what was known as "World's most unusual Drugstore."

DO IT IF: You harken back to a simpler time where there was 1 stop shopping and before CVS and Walgreens were on every opposite corner.

SKIP IT IF: You don't enjoy nostalgia, antiques or any reminders of the days gone by.

LOCAL ADVICE: Webb's City opened to the public in 1925 by James Earl "Doc" Webb as a small and modest storefront at the corner of 9th Street and 2nd Avenue South in St. Petersburg, Webb's motto was "Stack it high and sell it cheap." Webb's strong suit was getting thousands through the doors, with wacky attractions like dancing chickens, baseball playing ducks, a "live" mermaid show, a traveling circus in the parking lot, 3 cent breakfasts and more.

I DID IT: ☐   www.florida-backroads-travel.com/doc-webb.html

DID YOU KNOW?

At its peak, Webb's City expanded into a massive marketplace, featuring 77 different departments over 7 city blocks. While the attractions were a hit, the costs were a drag on profits. Webb's officially closed for good in, 1979. Sadly, the original building was knocked down in 1985.

ARRIVE AT
ANCLOTE KEY LIGHT

WHAT'S THE DEAL? If you are up for a challenge, this bucket list item is not easy to accomplish. If you are a lighthouse aficionado, you will find a way to make it happen.

DO IT IF: you want to see every lighthouse in Florida, no matter how difficult the challenge.

SKIP IT IF: You like lighthouses but they need to be easy to visit.

LOCAL ADVICE: Anclote Key is a remote barrier Island, roughly 3 miles off the shore from Tarpon Springs. There is no bridge or causeway to reach it, one can only arrive by boat, which is somewhat of a blessing. If you want to see what it's like to be on an almost deserted Island, Anclote Key is your spot. There are 4 Islands that k up the 11.000 acre preserve, and ferry service is available from the sponge docks I Tarpon Springs.

I DID IT: ☐ www.floridastateparks.org/Anclote-Key

DID YOU KNOW?

The lighthouse at the southern end of Anclote Key has served as a beacon to ships since President Grover Cleveland commissioned the tower in 1887. It was decommissioned in 1984, restored by Florida Park Rangers in the early 1990's and still maintained by the dedicated folks from the Park Service. The lighthouse was built and began operation on September 15, 1887. Today the lighthouse is maintained as a historic structure.

EAT LIKE YOU'RE IN ATHENS

WHAT'S THE DEAL? Try something new with a visit to the delicious ethnic restaurants you will find in Tarpon Springs.

DO IT IF: You are craving authentic Moussaka, Souvlaki followed by Baklava.

SKIP IT IF: It's all Greek to you.

LOCAL ADVICE: Picking the best Greek Restaurant in Tarpon Springs is almost like selecting your favorite child. They are really all wonderful, so you almost cannot make a poor choice. One we have personally samples is Hellas, which has served authentic Greek food since 1970. The souvlaki, chicken Kabobs and hummus were fantastic. And for those with a sweet tooth, they have an extensive bakery with of course, Baklava, OPA!

I DID IT: ☐ www.hellasbakery.com

DID YOU KNOW?

> With age-old recipes, Greek cuisine has been influenced by Middle Eastern, Italian, and Ottoman cultures. Fresh vegetables, fish, olive oil, wine, meat, and grains play a significant role in these dishes, as well as cheese, bread, olives, herbs, and yogurt.

100

TAKE A SPIN AROUND SUNSET

WHAT'S THE DEAL?   There is a wonderful, gulf front restaurant, where you can dine and get a full 360-degree view, without leaving your seat.

DO IT IF: You enjoy a full-service restaurant where you can also get a view of one of the wonders of nature.

SKIP IT IF: Spinning while you are dining aggravates your vertigo.

LOCAL ADVICE: Located 12 stories above the sand of St Pete Beach, you will find Spinnakers Rooftop Restaurant, on top of the Bellwether Hotel. You arrive by private elevator for a unique dining experience and will hardly notice the rotating room, until you notice the unobstructed sunset, directly from your table.

I DID IT: ☐   www.spinnersrooftopgrille.com

DID YOU KNOW?

The 12-story Bellwether Beach Resort was originally opened in 1975 as the Grand Plaza Hotel and remains, the tallest structure on St. Pete Beach. With such great views from Spinnakers, it is very popular, especially for Holidays, so reserve well ahead of time. You don't need to be staying at the resort to dine there.

Printed in Great Britain
by Amazon

24441273R00059